PICASSO

PICASSO:

RICK JACOBSON

SOUL ON FIRE

Illustrated by
LAURA FERNANDEZ
& RICK JACOBSON

TUNDRA BOOKS

The publisher extends sincere appreciation to the Estate of Pablo Picasso, SODRAC, Magmaphoto, and Superstock for permission to reproduce the paintings of Pablo Picasso:
Science and Charity – 1897, early oil painting, CS009568 – Archivo Iconografico, S.A. / CORBIS/MAGMA
The Tragedy – 1903, Oil on wood, National Gallery of Art, Washington, MA01511A – Francis G. Mayer / CORBIS/MAGMA
The Jugglers – 1905, Gouache on cardboard, Pushkin Fine Art Museum, Moscow, Photo 261-775 / SUPERSTOCK
Les Demoiselles d'Avignon – 1907, Oil on canvas, Museum of Modern Art, New York, Photo 262-2170 / SUPERSTOCK
Guernica – 1937, Oil on canvas, Reina Sofia National Museum Art Center, Madrid, CS008595 – Archivo Iconografico, S.A. / CORBIS/MAGMA
Girl with Boat (Maya Picasso) – 1938, Oil on canvas, Rosengart Collection, Lucerne, 0000360659-002 – BEIRNE BRENDAN / CORBIS SYGMA/MAGMA
Ceramic Owl – Photograph by Peter Willi, Photo 1330-1170 / SUPERSTOCK

Published in Canada by Tundra Books,
481 University Avenue, Toronto, Ontario M5G 2E9

Published in the United States by Tundra Books of Northern New York,
P.O. Box 1030, Plattsburgh, New York 12901

Library of Congress Control Number: 2003108639

National Library of Canada Cataloguing in Publication

Jacobson, Rick
Picasso : soul on fire / Rick Jacobson ; illustrations by Laura Fernandez and Rick Jacobson.

ISBN 0-88776-599-8

1. Picasso, Pablo, 1881-1973—Juvenile literature. I. Fernandez, Laura II. Title.

N6853.P5J33 2004 j709'.2 C2003-903696-0

We acknowledge the financial support of the Government of Canada through the Book Publishing Industry Development Program (BPIDP) and that of the Government of Ontario through the Ontario Media Development Corporation's Ontario Book Initiative. We further acknowledge the support of the Canada Council for the Arts and the Ontario Arts Council for our publishing program.

Medium of illustrations by Laura Fernandez and Rick Jacobson: oil on canvas

Design: K.T. Njo

Printed in Hong Kong, China

1 2 3 4 5 6 09 08 07 06 05 04

For Enrique

ACKNOWLEDGEMENT

With thanks to Trevor

Les Demoiselles d'Avignon

When young Pablo Picasso first painted *Les Demoiselles d'Avignon*, people were shocked. The style was so new that they couldn't understand it, let alone like it. Some even said it was monstrous and mad, a "horrible mess."

Now we know it was the work of a genius striving to show his subjects' emotions and feelings, rather than simply recording their existence. Over time people have accepted Picasso's way of speaking through his art. To "hear" him better, it helps to learn more about the artist himself.

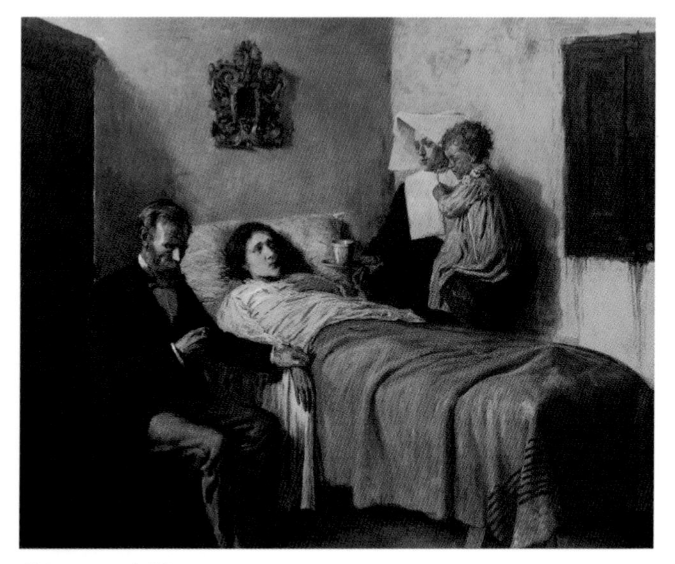

Science and Charity

Pablo Picasso was born in 1881 in the southern Spanish city of Malaga. His father, Don José Ruiz Blasco, was a painter who was particularly fond of painting doves and allowed Pablo to assist by finishing their feet. The child was an energetic student, filling countless sketchbooks with images of people and animals. By the time his son was eleven, Don José realized the boy's skill had surpassed his own. He handed Pablo his brushes and palette and gave up art for good.

When Pablo was only fifteen, he painted *Science and Charity*. (His father posed for the seated doctor.) The work told a story and recorded a moment in much the same way that photographs and movies commonly do now. This was an important purpose of art at the time, but it wouldn't hold Picasso's passion, or interest, for long.

The Tragedy

In his hands, Pablo's brushes were swift and charged with energy. The young prodigy rendered many of the same things that others did, but his intentions were far different. He wanted to express himself straight from the heart. And when his young friend, Carlos Casagemas, died in 1901, Pablo did just that. He was thrown into a state of melancholy. His work reflected his mood and so began Picasso's Blue Period. Canvases of unhappy, isolated people appeared again and again, in muted colors tinged with blue.

The Jugglers

The Blue Period lasted until late 1904, after Picasso had moved to Paris. There, he was in the company of other creative people and his spirits lifted. Once more, his emotional life crept into his paintings, which were now delicate and bathed in soft, warm, rose tints. The works of his Rose Period are lighter and filled with hope.

Sometimes inspiration is a difficult thing to come by. It hides when it is sought. When it is least expected, it appears. Picasso found inspiration by being open to it. One night he was at the home of writer Gertrude Stein when another talented painter and very good friend, Henri Matisse, arrived. He was carrying something that would change the course of Pablo's career again. It was a carved African head, and Picasso was enchanted. He held it all evening. He could not let it go.

Although Picasso continued in the "rose style," that carving obsessed him. It defined everything. It separated the different parts of the face and put them together in a new way. It was still a face, but it was so simplified that it was the *essence* of a face.

Quite often the ideas of one artist will inspire the work of another. Sometimes those ideas build, and a trend or movement begins. Paul Cézanne was one of the most famous artists of his time. When he died in 1906, an exhibition of his paintings was organized in Paris. Picasso studied the paintings carefully. Cézanne, too, had been influenced by African art. He had begun to explore ways of showing objects from several directions at once, almost as if he were walking around them. This concept, and the carved African head, sparked an idea in Picasso.

He ordered a huge canvas with extra reinforcing boards behind it for strength. The large painting – approximately eight feet square (244.9 x 233.7 cm) – was finished in the summer of 1907. It was called *Les Demoiselles d'Avignon*. One of the women's heads is clearly African, like the sculpture.

Les Demoiselles d'Avignon (detail)

When an artist produces a work that breaks the accepted fashion of the times, it is often received badly. This one, the critics and the public hated. It was even called a "loss to French art." Picasso felt so strongly about the painting that he didn't care about the comments. Instead, he continued to work, and a new style emerged that dominated his art for years. Simple things – a bottle, a glass, a guitar – were broken up and painted from several angles so the viewer could really "see" them. When he broke down what he saw, the images looked like sugar cubes. Cubism had been born.

Although gallery paintings may not be handled, they are full of textures, tastes, and smells familiar to the artist. One can imagine standing next to Picasso in his studio at 13, rue Ravignan in Paris. He called it the *Bateau-Lavoir*, or laundry boat. It was crowded with canvases, sketches, and props.

He would flex the stiff hog's hair brush against his palm, then swish it in a jar of turpentine. With a flick of his wrist he'd spray drops on the floor, then dip the brush into paint and begin. Picasso sketched compositions and details on paper ahead of time, but he rarely drew on the canvas. He rehearsed the images first and when he was ready, painted freehand, seeing the entire canvas as a whole. His paintings should be looked at in the same way.

Watch him now, squeezing jet-black paint onto his palette, tossing the tube onto the table, and looking for bright crimson. He grabs more different-sized brushes and holds them between his fingers. He attacks the canvas with fast, sure strokes. Where the paint is deep, he uses the brush handles to scrape into it. The man paints as if his soul is on fire. The paint is charged with energy.

Girl with Boat (Maya Picasso)

Looking at Picasso's art is about seeing the world through his eyes. Once he started breaking down what he saw, there was no limit. Eyes could roll to cheeks; a nose could slide off to the side. Yet the subject remained recognizable, perhaps more so than in a photograph.

From those early days of training with his father, Picasso had been able to draw brilliantly. He had not forgotten how. It was because he had such mastery of the rules that he could go beyond them.

Small finished ceramic owl

Picasso was a man of many emotions and sides. From his Blue to Rose Periods, through the Cubist revolution and into ceramics, collage, and sculpture, he led us on a marvelous tour. He even designed costumes and sets for a dance written by his friend Jean Cocteau. Through his art we not only learn about his life, but about his times and the events that affected him.

Between 1936 and 1939, a dreadful civil war raged in Spain. The fighting was long and bitter. On April 27, 1937, Picasso bought a newspaper and began to read it while he sipped his morning espresso. Then a headline caught his eye. Guernica, a small town near Barcelona, had been bombed and destroyed. Many innocent people had been killed in the horrifying attack of the undefended town.

Guernica

Picasso found himself back in his studio beginning work on one of his great masterpieces. His outrage is clear in this painting so full of symbols for us to read. His skill as a draftsman reveals his raw emotions. His ability to break the event apart describes the brutality of war.

For years Picasso insisted that *Guernica* could not go to Spain until the end of Fascism. It is now in the Reina Sofia National Museum Art Center in Madrid, where it is a prized national treasure.

Picasso lived to be 91 years old. In his long life he had four children. Many women loved him, and he married twice. Careful observers will see the skill and fierce intelligence behind his art. It is there in everything he touched. He changed the way we look at art.

Picasso created thousands of paintings. He would buy a house and paint until it was filled with canvases. Then he would lock it up and buy another. Unlocking those houses has revealed much about the man of action and towering brilliance. Through his art we can learn about his feelings, his life, his music, his passion. Best of all, we can open our own doors and find much about ourselves behind them.

PABLO PICASSO 1881 – 1973

1881 Pablo Picasso, the son of Don José Ruiz Blasco and Dona Maria Picasso y López, is born in Malaga, Spain on October 25. At first he appears to be stillborn, but his uncle, a doctor, blows smoke in his face, causing the infant to draw his first breath. This seems to be the first and last time Picasso lacked energy.

1896 At age 15, Picasso paints *Science and Charity.* He also passes his entrance examination at La Lonja School of Art (Escuela de Bellas Artes de La Lonja) in Barcelona. Although he is given a month, he completes his portfolio in only one day and outshines the graduating students.

1901 – 1904 (The Blue Period) When Picasso's friend Carlos Casagemas kills himself for love, Picasso begins a series of paintings dominated by the color blue. The sad theme of his work continues for three years.

1904 – 1907 (The Rose Period) A move to Paris, France and exposure to its lively arts community brings happiness back into Picasso's life. His works of this period are lighter, more delicate, and dominated with soft hues of rose. In 1906 famous artist Paul Cézanne dies. Picasso is fascinated by Cézanne's exploration of light and form. He also meets artist Henri Matisse, who becomes a lifelong friend.

1907 In Paris, Picasso goes to an exhibition of Cézanne paintings and is greatly influenced by it, as well as African sculpture. He paints *Les Demoiselles d'Avignon* and despite harsh criticism, the Cubist movement is under way. A new friend, Georges Braque, comes into his circle and joins the Cubist revolution.

1918 Picasso marries his first wife, Russian dancer Olga Koklova.

1921 Picasso's first child, Paul, is born.

1935 Picasso and Olga divorce and his second child, Maya, is born to Marie-Thérèse Walter.

1937 Picasso paints *Guernica* and sends it to the Spanish pavilion at the Paris World's Fair instead of his intended commission dealing with the theme "painter in studio."

1943 Picasso meets painter Françoise Gilot.

1947 Pablo and Françoise have a son, Claude.

1949 Picasso's early days of painting in bird feet for his father stand him in good stead when his *Dove* lithograph becomes the motif for the Paris World Peace Congress. When his fourth child, a girl, is born to him and Françoise in the same year, they name her Paloma, the Spanish word for "dove."

1961 At the age of 80, Picasso marries his second wife, Jacqueline Roque.

1967 Picasso refuses the French Legion of Honor.

1973 Picasso dies in France at the age of 91.

PIER
F. CHELFI
Le Monde
GUERNICA